"An expert on water conservation and supply, David Marquis has created a work that is both instructive and entertaining. No spoiler alert that the river always wins."

—Eric Nadel, Texas Rangers Radio Announcer, 2014 Ford C. Frick Award Recipient

"The timeliness of this book that reads with the rhythm of a musical composition is remarkable. *The River Always Wins* reminds us that just like the water in the river that *is*, we as humanity are *becoming*. Rising up and reborn as headwaters, collectively flowing through rapids, over sandbars, and around fallen trees, we are, nevertheless, moving toward the greater good—shaping the rock and transforming hearts along the way."

—Cynthia Seale, Trinity Waters

"I so appreciate David Marquis' spirit and determination. He once gave me a handprinted card that says: 'Be water, my friend.' David himself follows that concept, constantly flowing around corners and fearlessly leaping into the unknown to discover how to make the world a better bluegreen place to be."

—Jim Levitt, Fellow, Harvard Forest, Harvard University

The River Always Wins

David Marquis

*water
as a metaphor
for
hope and progress*

A LYRIC ESSAY

La
Reunion

Dallas, Texas

La Reunion Publishing, an imprint of Deep Vellum
3000 Commerce St., Dallas, Texas 75226

deepvellum.org · @deepvellum

DeepVellum is a 501c3 nonprofit literary arts organization founded in 2013 with the mission to bring the world into conversation through literature.

9781646050529 (hardcover)
978-1-64605-008-6 (paperback) | 978-1-64605-007-9 (ebook)

Support for this publication has been provided in part by
grants from the National Endowment for the Arts,
the Texas Commission on the Arts,
the City of Dallas Office of Arts and Culture's ArtsActivate program,
and the Moody Fund for the Arts:

LIBRARY OF CONGRESS CONTROL NUMBER: 2020932576

Cover design by Justin Childress | justinchildress.co
Interior Layout and Typeset by Kirby Gann

For Diana Navarrete Marquis, my wife

— a love that quenches like clear water —

But let justice roll down like waters, and righteousness like an everflowing stream.

AMOS 5:24, OLD TESTAMENT

Blest be the Streams from hills of snow,
     sweet be spring Waters unto thee.
Sweet be swift-running Waters, sweet to
     thee be Water of the Rains.

ATHARVAVEDA BOOK 19, HYMN 2
HINDU SCRIPTURE

ACKNOWLEDGMENTS

In 1995 when Ron Kirk became the first African American mayor in the history of Dallas, I wrote a poem for an inaugural event about a river that made its way to the sea.

That thought stayed with me and became the genesis for this book.

I would also like to acknowledge my good friend Bud Melton. Over a cup of coffee, he made a remark about the flow of water. Years later, his comment came back to me and sparked a theme in Chapter Six regarding floods and rapids. Thank you, Bud.

Decades ago I explored the work of the late novelist John Gardner. He wrote once of an exchange between a waitress and an old farmer during a drought in a small New England town. It's been so long that I don't even remember the characters' names, but the tone of their conversation has always stayed with me, given that I grew up in drought-stricken West Texas.

I want to acknowledge Becky Raider, naturalist extraordinaire, who supplied me with information about the age of the water in the Great Trinity Forest. Thanks as well go to Vikram Agrawal for his aid in deepening my understanding of Hindu scripture regarding water.

Many friends listened intently and with great passion as I read them Chapter One. Their responses tapped a deep well within me that led to the creation of this work. They include Eric Nadel, Betsy Del Monte, Keisha Whaley, Ruben Habito, Cynthia Seale, Andrea Ayvazian, Melanie Ferguson, John Matthews, Ben Mackey, Robin Sachs, Vynsie Law, Andy Sansom, Brent Brown, Willis Winters, Doug Wright, Steve Smith, Janice Bezanson, Molly Plummer, Robert Kent, Denise Lee, Scott Shirley, and many others. Lizbet and Adrien Palmer and Josh and Carlee Kumler provide emotional and spiritual support in ways they will never know.

I especially want to thank Garrett Boone, Trammell S. Crow, Claude C. Albritton, Jacques Vroom III, and Edwin Cabaniss for their support and encouragement.

Will Evans is not only a fine publisher but a skilled editor as well, and Clyde Valentin deserves thanks for introducing us. The cover illustration by Justin Childress grabbed me the moment I saw it, and Kirby Gann's design and layout are beautifully crafted.

Finally, I would like to thank my friend and colleague Neeki Bey, who read a first draft and said, "That's not it." He was right. He told me to keep writing and to pare the material down to its essence. This is the book that came from his wise words.

David Marquis
Dallas, Texas
April 2020

1

On a broad plain outside Taos, New Mexico, leading to the Sangre de Cristo Mountains, a bridge spans a deep, narrow gorge, and at the bottom of the steep rock walls is a river, the Rio Grande.

The water roaring below, so distant as to be silent in its rushing, did not begin its long journey to the Gulf of Mexico at the bottom of the gorge.

It began on the top, on the surface, and over more years than can be known—the way the indigenous know the time to plant corn or a mother knows to stroke a child's hair or even in the soulless counting of seconds within a digital timepiece—the water found and caressed and forced its way through rock. When the snow-melt ran plentiful, the water worked on the rock. When drought came, the water, though less, worked on the rock.

At no time did the water ever stop working on the rock. A single trickle, a single drop, constituted the whole of water itself, for its purpose and its nature are known to itself.

And what is the nature of the river?

The river is made of drops. Every river in the world—the Ganges, the Nile, the Hudson, the Amazon, the Mississippi—is made of drops. One drop is one drop is every drop.

Rivers, ancient as days, may differ in the life along their banks, their depth, or the frequency of their flooding, but one thing is true: if enough drops flow together in the same direction long enough, the river always wins.

There was a time in this country when black people were enslaved because of the color of their skin, but the river won.

There was a time when women were not allowed to vote, but the river won.

Through many centuries gay people had to live in the shadows and hide their truest selves, but the river is winning on that issue and will continue to.

If enough drops flow together in the same direction long enough, the river always wins.

2

The Drops

If you had enough people with enough eye-droppers, you could drain the oceans. One person after another stepping forward, bending down, filling their eyedropper, squeezing the contents into a bucket, passing the bucket back along an assembly line deep into the heartland where each bucket of salt water would be filtered through some kind of desalination device because, after all, you can't drink sea water or pour it onto crops.

It would be an altogether impractical and even futile undertaking, but you could do it.

It is possible because the ocean is made of the same building material as rivers. It is made of drops, and the drops of molecules. The drops, when gathered into a torrent, can either solve or create problems. A tsunami is a problem. A stream powering a gristmill to grind grain made it possible not only to eat but to store food.

We come from water, we evolved with water. Our ancient ancestors' brains had to adapt to and interact with the water around them, whether a Navajo in the desert or a Samoan on a Pacific island.

The ancients had no science, yet saw it, knew it. Understood.

To know the river, you have to understand the drops. Understand them.

The entire Pacific Ocean is nothing more than a collection of drops moving together like the liquid notes of an eternal symphony.

Water moves in this fashion because of its capacity for cohesion. The drops stick together.

Paint, for example, has adhesive properties. Additives cause it to adhere to wood and metal and plaster and Sheetrock, but the water, the most prevalent liquid in the paint, is cohesive by nature.

It sticks to itself. Beads of water are collections of drops. Sheets of water are collections of beads.

Water evaporates, or, with the slightest slant or angle, flows away. It goes on.

Cohesion provides power. When rains come and do not cease, causing rivers to rise and flood, people come together and form lines, handing sandbags one to the next to the next trying to protect the community. People become cohesive in order to stem the flood of cohesive drops. They take on the properties of water in order to hold back the water.

The river is coherent.

It is not only drops en masse that have power but the persistence of individual drops. One drop after another can not only wear away rock but can also keep us awake at night when dripping from a broken faucet or a thawing frozen pipe.

Is anything more annoying than a person — an activist, an agitator, or even a beloved child — who won't let go of an issue or a point of contention but keeps bringing it up over and over?

Throughout history, famous drops have persisted, irritating the powers that be — or were until enough drops deposed or exposed them — or fomenting change and in some cases going beyond change to revolution because they simply kept on dripping.

Big drops bring change.

Galileo
Joan of Arc

Rosa Parks

Mahatma Gandhi

Lech Walesa

Nelson Mandela

Dr. Martin Luther King, Jr.

Cesar Chavez

Susan B. Anthony

Harriet Tubman

Thomas Paine

Muhammad Ali

Jackie Robinson

These are the drops that, when forced up against the rock wall of injustice, bitterness, hatred, or even indifference, find a way through, over, or around in order to fulfill their purpose of moving on, of seeking and finding a path forward, powering through.

Some drops persist and become legendary. Others persist and while less renowned achieve eternal impact nonetheless.

One drop breaks free from the others, and, from the path it takes, draws others to itself.

It breaks free, and others follow.

In 1980 a Polish electrician named Lech Walesa climbed over a fence at the Gdansk shipyards and formed a trade union organization called Solidarity. Nearly a decade later, in November 1989, the Berlin Wall fell, and the Soviet Union slid downhill until its dissolution in 1991.

The drops have power. The insistence of their pinging, their refusal to stop, to be controlled or subjugated, is the genesis of their power.

Consider the dam. Dams do not break all at once. The last drop breaks the dam.

The first begins to wear it away.

Without the first, the power of the dam does

not erode. Cracks in the power structure neither take hold nor widen.

The same is true of our lives. The structures we put in place, from jobs to relationships — even marriages, for example — do not simply burst in a flood. They are more likely to wear away, one drop, one comment, one word said or unsaid, that erode the supposed permanence of the structure.

And when the dam fails, the river succeeds. The accumulation of coherent drops has won.

It has worn away the bulwark, and change rushes through.

The unyielding presence yields if enough drops gather and cohere. Their force will and must move forward.

They continue.

The drops ping and resonate as they fall. They gather.

3

The Rock

The harder the rock, the clearer the water.
The Mississippi River is called the Big Muddy
for a reason. It finds its way through some of the
richest farmland in the world. Here the water
absorbs land, and the land becomes water.

The soil giving way, crumbling and giving itself
to the water, was rock once. It is old, soft land
that morphs into the rich, brown gumbo of the
great north-south waterway from Minnesota
to the Gulf of Mexico—for soil is rock decom-
posed and deconstructed, squeezed, ground up
and ground down by vast ages of freeze and
thaw, of ice and melt over long, long periods of
contraction and expansion.

Clarity, sharp-eyed and certain of purpose,

comes from water passing over and cutting through hard rock.

We live on a rock covered mostly in water, spinning through space.

Living things cannot live without water, without quenching liquids. But together, plant and animal, quenched or not, we inhabit a rock.

You cannot stand on water. You cannot build on water. Unless you're Jesus, you can't walk on water. There has to be a firm surface somewhere.

Rock has purpose. There is a reason it exists. Without rock, the water has no form.

Rock is shape, it is form, structure, and solidity. It provides the walls of the canyon for the river to wear away, the raw substance in which it finds its course.

If the river has no rock to wear away, it will never reach the ocean. It will have no path. The water—the drops—must reach the ocean in order to join the Greater Water.

Every drop has a purpose. Its purpose is to interact with the rock in order to return to the Greater Water.

The harder the rock, the clearer the water.

Einstein taught that matter cannot be destroyed. It can change shape and be transformed but not destroyed. Gandhi taught that one of the central tenets of nonviolence is not merely to defeat one's adversary but to transform them.

As the water in a riverbed ripples past and washes over the underlying stones, a long process of transformation takes place. A particle of rock at a time sloughs off, gives way, and in so doing it becomes part of the river, it joins with the river and swims with the procession.

It does not transform the rock the way an old-time evangelist hopes to save souls with a dramatic altar call, with people streaming down the aisle to the front of the church to be saved in exorcisms of tears and heaving faith. No, it is a transformation of quiet, unceasing movement toward something greater than the self—transformation into a new form, in a far place, from a new form of movement.

The water simply keeps doing its job, keeps traveling toward the Greater Water, and in so doing washes away molecules and miniscule pieces, too small to be seen in the immediate, yet enfolding them in fluid and carrying them along.

The rock, this most solid of all things, becomes a shape shifter and glides away. Its matter does not disappear. It is transformed. Einstein and Gandhi come true in each moment in the movement to the sea. Einstein died in 1955, having suffered an abdominal aneurysm. Gandhi died in 1948, assassinated by a fundamentalist nationalist of his own faith.

Yet, wherever water flows over rock, the two live on.

In this way, the way of water transforming stone, we change. We change ourselves, and we change our cultures.

Only interactive forces can change one another. The rock changes because the water changes.

Enormous social change swept the globe in the second half of the twentieth century. The tsunami of economic expansion and social change that followed World War II brought with it rock 'n' roll and the civil rights movement, and then the women's movement, Chicano rights, gay rights, and environmentalism, all vast changes in social mores.

Laws changed as well. the Civil Rights Act,

The Voting Rights Act, Fair Housing, Equal Employment, Clean Air and Clean Water, the Environmental Protection Agency.

Birmingham, 1963. Police dogs and fire hoses and beatings and the blood of peaceful protesters running in the streets. Four little black girls killed in a church on a Sunday morning. Domestic terrorism. That was rock, it was hard, and hearts harder.

The water, and the blood, ran clear.

Dr. King wrote his "Letter from Birmingham Jail," insisting that the movement move forward without delay, that the river of freedom continue to flow to the Greater Water.

Laws changed, and our society changed. Some hearts changed as well, but not all.

Changing hearts is the hard part.

The only thing harder than rock is the human heart when left unchallenged and unchanged.

Not even a hard head compares with the intransigence of a hardened heart.

How many times does a heart beat in a lifetime? If one lives to be eighty, the heart of an eighty-year-old will have beaten more than three billion times in that one lifetime.

The flow of blood is like the flow of water, coursing on its way.

A shift from a rural economy and culture to an urban and suburban way of life, desegregation of public schools, an exploding divorce rate, the changing role of women in our society, the expansion of pharmaceutical and chemical industries, increased international trade and commerce, the emergence of digital technology, and the resegregation of schools.

That is a flood of change.

It is one thing to change a law. It is another altogether to change hearts.

We clearly changed many laws, and many lives were swept up and carried along.

Just as obvious is that many hearts remained as hard as stone. Racism persists. Homophobia. Sexism. Ageism. Violence.

We will not change hearts through argument or angry rhetoric. Name-calling and vitriol will not heal the wounds of terror and mass shootings. Nor will time simply, miraculously heal all wounds.

Time is an element in the healing process but is not the process itself. So is talking and listening and the transcendent power of love and forgiveness, the fluidity that rolls over us and bathes us like the water of the womb. Such stem from our humanity.

So too does our humanity add in hatred and jealousy and greed and darkness, yet the water washes it away.

The rock and the water live in tense harmony every day. They feed on the struggle. The rock stands the course of the river. And the water, its energy liquid and raw, cleans the rock and transforms it.

Harder and clearer, these elements coexist on a molecular level.

Our lives, and our politics, are much the same in terms of rock and water needing each other.

The water moves on, but the rock never makes it to the Greater Water. Only if it gives of itself a little at a time can any part of it move forward.

It might stand strong holding its ground, but that ground never moves, it stands only in one place, seeing the same thing, the same vista, every moment of every day, looking in one direction only.

Our lives, and our politics, are much the same in terms of rock and water needing each other. So do we require one another on a molecular level.

The Vietnam War split one nation and laid waste to another. In America it rent asunder families, especially, it seems, fathers and sons. But somehow they now have reconciled, those wounds still healing.

A young boxer named Cassius Clay changed his name to Muhammad Ali and became a drop of water pushing for peace and was widely derided and suffered the slings and arrows of the same crowd that once cried, "Barabbas!" yet by the end of his life was cherished, The

Champ to all. The old accusations and blames had melted away. He died beloved by the world. Hardened hearts had reached a softer place.

Hope moves on. It has to.

4

The Headwaters

It is the headwaters of movement, for all activity on the earth is tied to the movement of water, of tides, of rivers and rainfall, of drinking water moving through pipes, of crops and hydro power, of wild animals on the Serengeti migrating to watering holes, and that movement, the movement of water, is tied to gravity and slope and the moon, and the moon to the earth and the earth to the sun and to the far reaches of the universe.

The clear liquid raised to your lips in a simple glass comes not only from a faucet or a well but from the dark side not only of the moon but the cosmos itself.

Creation myths from around the world often

feature water. The old narrative, the testament from the desert home of the Judeo-Christian tradition, begins with Genesis 1:1. The text says that the Spirit of God was moving over the face of the waters.

It was moving. It had somewhere to go.

In Hinduism, the Ganges is sacred. The River Styx is the crossing point into the afterlife in Greek mythology.

In these beginnings was water, seminal in our understanding of starting points, of crossings and endings.

The goddess of the sea in Pacific Island traditions rises from the ocean and brings abundance and blessings.

In the newer narrative, Jesus, while wandering in the desert, dealt with water over and over—he walked on it, turned it into wine, was baptized in it, bathed people's feet with it, and referred to it throughout his teachings, such as the story of the woman at the well.

The headwaters are not only physical and measurable in terms of flow rates and volumes but are present as well in the spiritual lives of people all over the world.

Whole cultures rise up, the manifestations both spiritual and physical, from the narrative of water understood and made real in place and time. From the beginning they are with us.

Headwaters, whether bubbling up from a muddy seep or rippling in a thin sheet down a rock face, seek a place to go, to pool resources and organize into a trickle and then a stream, carving and curling down an arroyo toward a creek and then a tributary to find a canyon, always seeking, always wanting.

What, then, are headwaters? They are a place

to prepare, not simply to begin, but to make ready, to gather strength and sense of purpose.

Headwaters do not simply rise up out of the ground in an instant. Science can now provide carbon dating for water, can determine the age of water in a particular place.

A spring in Dallas, Texas, recently became of interest. It rose up out of the ground near the Great Trinity Forest, the largest urban forest in America. Testing demonstrated that the water in the spring was almost a thousand years old. And as it bubbled up to the surface it was reborn. Given new purpose. Seeking a new way.

There is no new water.

An element of water's magic, its hold on us, is its ability to renew us, whether a long draw on a tall glass on a hot day or a dip into a pool.

But none of that water is new. It is new to us

at that moment, but its headwaters, the beginnings of each drop, are ancient. It is old but makes us new again.

It is a thread that ties us to the human narrative all the way back to the first humans. Blessed be the tie that binds, and that tie is water.

It is widely thought that the venerable Rosa Parks and her refusal to give up her seat on the bus in Montgomery, Alabama, in December of 1955, are the headwaters of the American civil rights movement. But the headwaters of that river came long before.

On the west coast of Africa more than 400 years ago, there was a human being in chains, standing, looking out onto water, vast and distant: the Atlantic Ocean. They saw the ships, their sails, knew their purpose. Slave ships, ready.

From somewhere within them rose up the words, "Oh, hell, no." And then, "We will be free. And if not us, then our children, our children's children, the grandchildren of our grandchildren. We will be free."

Oh, hell, yes.

The headwaters are within us. There is no new water.

Water's age reminds us that while humans may sometimes engage in spontaneity, nature rarely does. Evolution, gestation, adaptation, the change of seasons, life cycles, planting, tending, and harvesting, not only take time, they require time. They insist on it. Though certain human endeavors involve spontaneity, many do not.

Some that seem spontaneous are the least so. When an actor bursts into song during a musical as the music swells, it is the product of countless hours of rehearsal. The smoother the scene, the more preparation went into it.

It is this sense of time that causes us now to apply technology to water. Mother Nature has for millennia filtered water through natural processes. Rain falls, is filtered through grasses and over tree roots and works its way through rock and soil and earth, and finally gathers underground until ready to reemerge as headwaters. But our human population has grown now so that nature can no longer supply water to humans quickly enough to keep up with demand.

Filtration is the future of water. Wetlands constructed by humans, filtration systems such as direct potable reuse, desalination, all are needed and will be increasingly necessary as more people populate the earth and more distillates and tiny fibers of tires and brakes find their way into waterways.

We have simply overwhelmed Mother Nature's timetables and capacity for filtering our most precious resource.

Our headwaters were previously always water derived from natural processes but now of necessity must be altered by manmade chemicals and mechanical products of filtering screens so small that a human hair will not pass through them.

In this sense, in the use of technology to clean water and to monitor the use and conservation of water, we stand at our own headwaters, the beginnings of a river of innovation that we must now have of our own creation just to manage our way out of our own mismanagement. We stand at the headwaters now.

In Minnesota, where it comes up out of the earth, you can step over the headwaters of the Mississippi.

Will we ever be able to step over the headwaters of the polluted river of our own making, its banks so wide, its water so dirty?

All innovation springs from its own headwaters, from the filtered and gathered drops of all that has come before it.

All require preparation of sorts, each of its own kind, each from its own headwaters.

Headwaters do not suddenly spring up out of the ground. They come from a long period of gathering, a gathering of drops. The headwaters are in essence a harvest, a harvest of drops like a harvest of grain.

The headwaters are both planting and harvest, the gathering of seeds into a chorus ready to sing.

5

The Course of the River

Rivers do not run in straight lines. Neither do our lives.

The shortest distance between two points is a straight line, but rivers do not bother with geometry. They create their own, carving shape out of resistance, from that which resists them.

The river is an artist, raising its hammer and chisel, sculpting its way to the art of its bed, finding the shape of the rock that is its own course, for no two rivers in the world run the same.

Neither do our lives. Carving life, chiseling the riverbed, the course of an artist and an activist. Three main issues along the path: education, the environment, and human rights. Write. Perform. Create change. Listened to my mother, who did much good in the world. She said that protesting was not enough. You have to make it real. Make it last. Change laws. Do the hard work of organizing new structures and winning people over to your side through persuasion and persistence. Listened. Rejected shape and strictures and limits and found a path to a river headed for a better, more just place.

Shape be damned. Movement. If it serves the course of the river, movement defines shape and creates its own.

The course of the river is a lesson in the necessity of place and with it the imperative and the ability to adapt. The lush forestation of the Shenandoah Valley both requires and provides a rich diversity of wildlife and plant species while the chalky shallow bed of the White River in West Texas provides a sight line to a vast, distant horizon and a muted palette of plant and animal life seen and known only by lovers of arid lands.

Such linear choices of bodies of water are lessons in diversity. Much has been made of diversity. It has become corporate and political, packaged and sold, discussed and debated, and, in the same moment, welcomed by some and resented by others.

If you seek diversity, look to nature. The natural world, over courses of ages so long they are hard to count and harder to comprehend, adapted. It had to, to survive, and then to flourish.

Look to nature. There the diverse and adaptable abound, though threatened now by the promulgation of one species, the one on two legs, unsure sometimes of where it is going.

The Trinity River runs south and east from north and west of Fort Worth through Dallas all the way to Houston and the Gulf of Mexico. Almost half of the population of Texas gets their water from its watershed. It seems to be clear on where it is going, but on the southern edge of Dallas, it suddenly loops back as though it has changed its mind, heads briefly to the north, and then resets its course, looping south once more and going on its way.

The river goes where it can, and then, once it has amassed enough power, where it will.

Along its way, the river provides, it gives of itself, its services, quenching and nurturing and transporting, but it is not here for us.

It has its own somewhere to go, to run its own course, and we can go with it or not, but whether we choose to travel with it, or not, it will travel its course.

It lends drinking water and sustains crops, offers its banks for economic development, carries barges and stimulates commerce, opens its arms to recreation and fishing.

Yet none of those are the reason the river runs. Its singular purpose is to traverse its course until it reaches the Greater Water, to leave the watershed where it began and move on.

That is the course of the river, to constantly leave itself, to move on by leaving behind.

The river goes somewhere. Here is not it. Here is not where. It is there, someplace other than here.

Watersheds, diverse and adaptive, write themselves into the earth, for water must have a means to leave the land.

In order to do so, to be true to its relentless self, it must do four things:

Seek, choose, continue, and persevere.

So, too, our lives.

To seek and to desire the searching and to accept it.

To choose in the etching and sculpting and hammering and chiseling the very course one hammer strike at a time.

To continue, continue.

To persevere from the necessity of place to the endless destination.

That is how a drop makes it to the sea, to the Greater Water.

Much has been made of the journey, the path, the simple going.

But it is the pathfinding that matters.

It is the gravity and slope and density and

diversity of rock and trees and living things and beaver dams and sandbars and snags and obstacles and shifts in direction that rivers cope with and adjust to each day.

So do we, and we find these obstacles precisely because of our pathfinding. Finding the obstacles, overcoming the obstacles, even welcoming them, is part of the reason we go.

Finding the path is blazing the path is traveling the path in order to be farther along when the sun falls into the evening.

The rolling conjoined coherent force of drops has somewhere to be, and here isn't it.

Here is not that somewhere.

The somewhere to go and to be once there is the water seeking itself, of water seeking other water and its larger self, drops finding drops, it seeks itself, its own greater self, its source and its renewal, where it comes from and where it is going, its leaving.

Going nowhere is impossible. We are each always going somewhere, even if only inching toward death.

They go, rivers do.

They go some other place than here and not toward death.

Water values movement.

Movement is life. The drops are moving with purpose, and there is a destination involved.

It is relentless. The drops are forceful.

That is how the drops together make it to the sea. The daily work.

The river takes care of its business and expects us to do the same.

Rivers do not wander for the sake of aimlessness.

Even when they wander, they go.

Its movement is intentional, for it intends to wash away the rock.

The only path laid out for it is the path of doing the daily work, of washing away the rock, but the river still has to do that work in order to move.

It seeks itself, the river does. The river seeks itself.

It is not the path of least resistance. It is the path of opportune resistance, for rivers do not adhere to the clean lines of geometry.

They do get out of their banks, often in times of floods. Of excess. They can change course or widen or deepen their channel. Times of earthquake, million-year rains, or cataclysmic change. And it is in those times of change that we need to be most ready for extremes, for excess or lack and the lessons that come with them.

6

Rapids and Floods

Water brings life. Too much water brings death. Too much water: rapids and floods. They are different, these two.

The rapids are the same water in less space. A flood is more water in the same space.

Both are instructive.

We learn what we can handle, learn the difference between exhilaration and fear.

We learn when to step in and when to withdraw, learn limits.

Both can edify. Both can kill.

Consider a gallon of water. Eight pounds, a gallon of water weighs eight pounds. How many gallons are there in a torrent, a wall of water?

Water is life-giving for we are born of fluid, but make no mistake: the same life liquid that sustains us also washes cars away, sweeps houses off their foundations, drowns us, pummels us, overtops levees, sweeps the unsuspecting out to sea, blows out dams, capsizes boats, inundates cities, gathers into tsunamis, and deals death and destruction with fury, but never with ego or ill will.

We are living on its planet, and sometimes we simply get in the way.

Nothing personal.

Nothing personal at all.

It is not our planet, after all.

We're just visiting, and nature knows it.

While we are here, we must learn to deal with excess, with times of deluge, when water comes at us, or when we shoot through the rapids set before us.

I know floods, saw them in the sky, floods of dust. Growing up on the plains of West Texas in the crushing drought of the 1950s, walking home from school backward to keep the sand and grit out of our eyes, the wind howling, the sun obscured from the sky at three o'clock in the afternoon, the dust storms flooded our homes, our lives, the town. The sky was full of drops, each grain of grit and dust and sand a drop, whipping through the sky, scouring its way across the ocean of land.

A flood cuts wide.

A rapid cuts deep.

You can choose to live in a floodplain, but you cannot choose when the flood will come or how damaging it will be. Either accept the choice and live with the risk, or know that such a place is not for you and move on. Rebuild and take out more flood insurance? Or distance yourself? Is it worth it, the sounds and scents of all those cohesive drops, all that life flowing close, cutting its way through rock, worth the risk?

A flood cuts wide. A rapid cuts deep.

You can choose whether to shoot the rapids, and you can choose whether to portage your canoe. You can choose your gear and your guide. But you do not get to choose where the boulders are. You can only know that they are there and prepare accordingly.

The power of a flood is that it is unchanneled, unbridled. The power of rapids is that it is a test, a show of force, of will.

Children at a birthday party, high on sugar, are a flood. One teenager is rapids.

The channeling of energy brings direction and purpose. Not channeling such energy is a form of death because it is a form of waste. The challenge of excess is to focus the energy and power of the drops and organize them to move through difficult times and spaces.

It is the difference between a riot and a movement.

Dust storms were a flood. Wind energy is a movement.

A riot will wear itself out. A movement moves on. It goes through its confined spaces, its tumult, its uproar, its aeration and oxygenation, rousting and cleansing itself.

The Stonewall pushback at a bar in New York

in the summer of 1969 was an uprising. The gay rights river that flowed from it was a movement.

The election of Ronald Reagan in 1980 by huge margins was a flood on the right. The conservative river that sprang forth flows on today.

Floods lay waste to lives and property and leave us asking if we can benefit or learn from them in any way.

All floods ask questions. The rush of chemicals into the bloodstream of an alcoholic or an addict leaves desperate family members wondering how many more times they will have to check a father or mother, a sister or brother into rehab. Floods of emotion. Of energy. Despair. Depression. Maybe joy, sooner or later.

Floods come upon us. Rapids appear before us.

The flood comes to us. We go to the rapids.

You know where they are, where they begin, where they end.

The rapids provide clear evidence of the power, the usefulness, of channeling energy.

If you can survive the rapids, you can move swiftly down the river.

The flood abates.

The rapids continue.

You choose to go into the rapids

For the energy.

The challenge.

The absolute exhaustion.

The thrill, heart racing, adrenaline pumping.

You know where it ends.

Go down into the rapids with respect and trep-
idation, and if you make it through, you've
accomplished something.

To make it to the Greater Water, you either
have to shoot the rapids or get out and carry
your canoe.

You choose to get out of the flood because you
know you are overwhelmed.

> Up to higher ground.
> Climb to higher ground.
> Scramble and clamber.
> Out of fear or acknowledgement or
> simple recognition that you are over-
> matched.

The flood has served you well. It has caused
you to move to higher ground. From there you
can see the river, can see what lies ahead.

Do not sacrifice yourself to the raging waters, to floods of panic and emotion, for you will never reach the Greater Water. When life overwhelms you, get to higher ground!

Every drop, including you, is needed to continue moving the river to the Greater Water. The flood will pass. This, too.

A flood of intolerance and hatred has come upon us. It waited in the sky, gathering in storm clouds for many years. Now its dark weight has fallen to the earth.

Study the river. Know it. Its every turn, every sandbar and eddy, is your salvation or your death.

The Greater Water awaits, but the rapids lie in between.

Seek higher ground! We choose to be swept away, to participate in and drown in the flood if we do not.

From there we can see the rapids, study the boulders and the roiling waters, see the bend in the course.

Study the river. Know it.

The rapids propel the drops to the Greater Water.

You can try to hold back the flood, but you will lose. It is greater than you, more powerful. You will not withstand it. Prepare instead for the rapids and go on.

When you don't see them coming, the rapids slam you. Study the river. Come to still water.

7

Still Water

There is an old saying that still water runs deep, but that is not true.

If it ran, it wouldn't be still.

Water will slow when emerging from a rapids or after a flood, move a bit in one direction or another, but it is never still, for the earth is not flat, because gravity is always pulling at it. Because nothing alive is ever still, and water is very much alive.

Nothing is ever still on a molecular level, not within us and not on the far edges of the universe, ever expanding and pushing on and hurtling away from itself and ourselves.

The rapids and the flood exhaust us, make us cry out for respite and rest. Stillness washes us up on the bank, gasping and coughing up the torrent that has overwhelmed us.

Movement will continue. The water wants to go on, but sometimes it must rest.

Water at rest—a pond, a pool, Lake Placid— calms the soul. It brings peace.

After the movement and struggle of a march or a protest, Mahatma Gandhi would return to the ashram, to his home, to feed the goats, spin yarn on his spinning wheel, and spend time with the children of the community. Many times Jesus walked away from the crowds that followed him to go into the mountains to pray, to seek stillness. The Buddha sought relief from the suffering world and found an Enlightened Path.

Oh, how we long to be still.

People fight their way through traffic, an hour commute each way to work, listening to music, audiobooks, or podcasts while in the car. When pressed, they say that being alone in their car in the crush of traffic is their only time to themselves all day, their alone time, their vespers.

Solitude in rush hour, a drop bobbing on a river of traffic, flowing with other drops down a concrete riverbed.

And after work? Rush home, change into expensive yoga gear, and drive like hell to make it to class to study an ancient tradition that offers mindfulness and inner peace.

Oh, how we long to be still.

What happens within still water, the liquid in a pond? What of the life within it? What happens to and in the water?

Still water is not stagnant. Still water is full of

plant and aquatic life, home to life and growth. It is never stagnant because there is life beneath the surface—fish, bacteria, frogs, snakes, oxygen, sunlight.

Consider the infant, asleep in the crib. They seem still, but inside, below the surface, a mind-boggling number of cells are multiplying and splitting and reproducing and growing at a pace we can barely comprehend.

With water, with people, the good stuff is below the surface.

Snorkeling once off an island in the Philippines, the ocean surface calm, but beneath it—ah!—life! Fish in all shapes and sizes and stripes and colors!

When water is no longer alive below the surface, then it becomes stagnant. Humanity has the capacity to pollute living water, to deaden it: to set fire to the Cuyahoga River, or create a dead zone in the Gulf of Mexico. Or we can clean up our own mess, make our waters alive and well, and with them, ourselves, for still water renews. It breathes, a process of renewal.

The Zen master, when asked the essence of Zen, offers three words: *Catch your breath.*

Breathe and know that you are breathing. Breath and stillness are serious business, the essence of life, of survival, and yet they play together like the raised consciousness of children.

Raised consciousness brings a return to a natural pace, free from the compressed space of the rapids and from the chaos of flood.

We have come to live in a flood of constant stimulation, our fingers moving across the screens of our devices, images leaping from the screens into our eyes. Desiring to be still but never still, we chase after it, throw money at it.

Perhaps we can no longer be still, can only buy it an hour at a time. Or we turn to ancient texts. The scripture says, be still and know that I am God. The atheist might say, be still and know that there is no God.

But be still in any case at any time! Catch your breath.

Is a runner ever more still, more conscious, than when they are running? They run to become still, the stride, the motion of the arms, the breath, the escape from home and office and freeways and the assault of images.

Swimmers find stillness in the water, the repetition of strokes and the constancy of breathing.

Is a racecar driver ever more still than when they are zooming around a track? Is the Sufi dancer ever more still than when whirling in countless circles? In their whirling they find a way to be still, to be in a place and in a frame of mind to shut out all else so that nothing else matters.

The ballerina, leaping through the air, landing, turning again and again, is focused, fully engaged and alive.

Move and be still. The trick is to be still while in motion.

Create stillness.

In a darkened theater.

In a sleep-inducing sound machine.

The sound of rain.

The sound of the womb.

Of the ocean.

Of water lapping softly against a boat.

Let there be quiet.

The richness of stillness.

The world today is a constant flood of stimulation, and humanity goes to great lengths to get away from it or pays to watch others who excel at finding stillness while moving. Yoga and meditation and mindfulness are revered practices, and they have become industries. Vision quests were once the sacred practices of indigenous peoples and now are the pursuit of those with money to burn.

One can be still or one can pursue stillness, but in the end, stillness must reside within.

One becomes still in order to move forward, to continue to the Greater Water. Living life at flood stage expedites the journey, but it will do damage along the way. It cannot be sustained.

Being busy has become equated with being

important, as though the value of a human being is based upon how busy they are.

Being busy doesn't make you special. It just makes you busy. And tired.

Behold the busy man, justifying his existence on the planet with his busy-ness, measured by the amount of dust he kicks up each day, by the amount of material goods he consumes at all hours of the day and night.

In prior times, not that long ago, stillness came each day when the sun went down. It was imposed by the simple setting of the sun, by light and dark, and gave way with the advent of electricity. Yet in many places in the world, the electrical grid is still unreliable. While some on the planet are able to choose a sort of stillness as they sit before a glowing light — from their television, computer, phone — others find stillness imposed on them by unbroken darkness.

Only a generation ago, there was a day—Friday for Muslims, the Jewish Sabbath from sundown Friday to sundown Saturday, and Sunday for Christians—when most people were still. People's lives and jobs were hard, physically demanding, and a day of rest at week's end beckoned the weary, resting from the physical labor and strain of daily life. Rest was good. Now people choose to run marathons, bicycle indoors without going anywhere, and pick up heavy weights, then put them back down where they found them, all to overcome the terrible strain of sitting all day at work.

Some do not sit. They kneel. The devout Muslim stops five times a day to pray, answering the call to prayer from the muezzin. Stepping off an elevator in a hotel in Peshawar, Pakistan, in that place to study freedom movements and interview members of the Afghan mujahideen when they were fighting the Soviets, stepped into a hallway full of Muslim men on their prayer rugs facing Mecca. Remembered raucous fundamentalist revivals in my native West Texas, Hindu festivals in India brimming with ecstatic dance and bursts of color, and reverential Masses in Latin in cathedrals in New York, but those Muslim men on their knees, their faces bent to the carpet, made an impression. In a hotel hallway in the middle of the afternoon, they were still.

As with the activity beneath the surface of still water, the inner life of the spiritual practitioner offers respite and oxygen, and, when fully alive, the heart fully open, a diversity of life forms.

Stillness is not an end, it is a means to prepare the inner life and open one's heart enough to move on to the Greater Water, to rest in order to be able to deal with the remainder of the journey. The rapids and the flood are not the hardest part, only the quickest. Just as the excess of flood and rapids requires rest and recovery, so too must one prepare for what is to come.

The swimmer's breath, the runner's heart-beat, must return to normal after a race. So too does the river need to recover after the rapids. The river reengages with itself. When going through the rapids, there is no time to be introspective or to ponder new life. The growth only comes if one survives it and becomes stronger because of it.

Even when the still water is replenished and the life beneath the surface has found the calm goodness and fulfilling richness of achieving stillness, it must yet be restored on a regular basis by the addition of new water. More water must come in order to maintain the water level because water moves not only through the course of the river but into and through the sky as well. Evaporation is ever present, and does what it does, taking water, moving it, a never-ending cycle of extracting and replenishing. On an average summer day in a hot climate, a lake or reservoir will lose as much water to evaporation as to usage in all its forms—drinking, bathing, cooking, irrigation of lawns and trees, swimming pools. All its uses and forms are matched by the power of the sun and the natural processes of the planet.

The water simply goes away into the sky, and when it does not fall again in the same place for some time, the lake levels drop, the ponds dry up, the riverbed aches.

There is no new water, and the earth is large enough to take and to give in unexpected places—drought in Texas can take place at the same time that floods besiege North Carolina.

It does not go away for good. It just moves around. It just goes away for a while.

Still water becomes a quieter place as fish die and aquatic plants wither. Quiet water begets silent land—parched, split open, grieving, the livestock bawling from thirst, the sun relentless.

Drought has come, has arrived like a teacher intent on lessons.

8

Drought

God bless drought. Without it, we would all die of thirst.

Drought is a teacher, flinty and weathered. It cares not a whit for self-esteem or the student's feelings. Either learn from it or not.

When offered such lessons, one has a choice. Learn from it once—the first time—or learn it again and again.

What to do? What to do?

The river has come through the rapids and survived the flood. The drops have rested and rejuvenated in the still water and are ready to move on to the Greater Water.

But there is no water, for drought has come.

Look to the sky. Pray for rain. Do a rain dance. Seed the clouds. Curse the weather forecaster. All of that, and still no rain.

Floods don't take long. Even a short drought lasts forever.

Dust kicks up, and the air is hotter than the day before. A hawk falls from the sky, dead before it hits the ground, dehydrated. Squirrels come to bury their faces and suck droplets out of a faucet in the yard while blue jays squawk and fuss, waiting their turn. Fish flop among the parched rushes and die, and the bleached rib cages of the fallen litter the dry earth as stark testament to the killing power of the land when betrayed and abandoned by rain that refuses to fall. Livestock in the field bawl, their stock tanks gone to powdered soil as the wild ones move from watering hole to shriveled creek bank to the trickle left in the river bed.

As long as there is water in the river, it will move toward the Greater Water.

At no time does the water ever stop working on the rock. When drought comes, the water, though less, works on the rock.

The lessons of drought: Filter it. Conserve it. Change. Adapt. Create new water-wise technology—dishwashers and washing machines, showerheads and toilets. Today we have new tools, new technology. A farmer can look to his phone to examine data gathered by satellite and determine if a particular field on his farm needs water, then can irrigate that one parcel more efficiently than ever before. These are drops of change. They are welcome, but humanity needs a long soaking rain of both goodness and goodwill on a global scale.

The Romans built aqueducts. The ancestors developed ceramics to haul and store water. They dug wells, and now we drill them.

Still there is no way to defeat a drought. It will rain when it wants to. But there is a way to survive one.

Learn the art of defiance.

Hope and patience and progress are beautiful and uplifting and sustaining and grow from open hearts and faithful spirits, yet the art of defiance stands just behind them, scarred and keen on battle. It refuses to die and bends only of necessity and not for long. By God it will not be broken and stands behind hope like a big brother just off the bus and looking for a fight, more than happy to join in and throw a few punches. The art of defiance lights the candle of hope with a blowtorch and a chip on its shoulder.

An old rancher in South Texas survived the drought of the 1950s, second worst only to the Dust Bowl of the Great Depression. The land had been in his family for generations, so he had no debt, no threat from the bank. A year passed with no rain. Another and another. He sold off his herds, kept his favorite saddle horse and one milk cow. Seven years. No rain. Asked how he handled it, he offered two words:

"I waited."

Nelson Mandela waited twenty-seven years in a jail cell in South Africa.

Off the Cape of Good Hope at the southern tip of Africa stands Robben Island, where he was imprisoned, where two great oceans come together, the Atlantic and the Indian, clanging forces of water. So too did powerful forces clash around Mandela, one seeking change and reconciliation, the other resisting change with drought-stricken hearts.

When Mandela finally got out of jail, he made it rain. It rained freedom, and it rained joy. He went around the world on a speaking tour, filling stadiums with hundreds of thousands of full-throated supporters whose vocal outpourings were the chiming bells of liberation and led to the downfall of apartheid in South Africa that had once seen five million people rule twenty-five million at gunpoint.

He went up against forces greater than himself, paid a dear price for it, then became his own greater force, and died a legend and a global hero. He turned drought into a thunderclap of approbation.

Those who live through the great droughts, whether of rain or money or incarceration, never forget it. Some never got over the Dust Bowl and Depression of the 1930s. They kept bits of food wrapped in foil in the freezer just in case they ever had to stare down hunger again.

Hope does not merely help us make it to and through the future but teaches us the value of that which we have already learned.

Do we learn it the first time, or must we learn it again and again? The Dust Bowl was not only caused by a lack of precipitation but also by misguided economic policies that encouraged farmers to plant every square inch of their fields, encouraged the plowing up of the short grass prairie. These poor decisions and worse policies brought the howling dust as much as nature did. Our part, the part we play in bad decisions that lead to financial collapse or environmental calamity, is exactly that. Our part. Our responsibility.

The lone candle lighting the darkness has to be about more than hope and patience and humility. It has to be about accepting responsibility, finding a better way, developing better methods of soil conservation, planting rows of trees as windbreaks, crop rotation, letting fields lie fallow sometimes, and looking ourselves in the eye when it comes to acknowledging our role in wreaking havoc upon the earth and ourselves. Drought settles in for a long stay when our own lack of planning or insipid decisions invite the forces of nature to unpack their bags and make themselves at home.

It is excess that leads to drought: climate change; the housing bubble of 2008; the stock market crash of 1929.

The market forces of excess are simply human beings acting in concert with one another. Or a lack thereof.

Lack is tied directly to excess. A lack of foresight, a lack of planning, a lack of thinking, all conjoin to become a force greater than ourselves, become a wall of dust barreling down out of the western sky scouring everything in its path. The same is true now of hurricanes made ever more fierce by rising ocean temperatures brought on by change brought on by excess.

Will we learn? The art of defiance includes defying our baser instincts and then calling ourselves and each other up to higher ground and higher standards.

Forces greater than one person include the force of two people—two drops—committed to staying in the river, of never ceasing to work on the rock, of pushing on to the Greater Water.

It is waiting. The Greater Water is waiting, just as it did for the ancestors, calling them to create tools and overcome diseases, to pursue science, to refuse war and move beyond savagery, and to establish humane systems of governance. To overcome themselves. To overcome ourselves.

All of that, plus the guts to ride it out.

Hardened, leathered faces search the sky for a hint of rain. "We got some weather," they say, meaning they got a storm, got some precip.

Today there are not only flash floods but also a new concept: flash droughts, when the ground has been so long without water and become so dry, the ground so broken, the fissures deep as a farmer's hand, and then the rain comes, blessed water from the sky! And it all runs off. The land does not absorb it. The next day the fissures are still there. The drought is back in a flash.

Economies experience drought, cycles of excess and lack, never learning the lessons of scarcity.

Marriages experience drought, sometimes so broken that no amount of love and therapy can heal the fissures.

In baseball, batters experience drought and go into a slump, can't buy a hit. They watch video of their swing, put in extra time in the batting cage, but still they bite at the low and away pitch, their humanity overcoming their training. Sometimes we are overwhelmed by too much or too little and cannot explain it. We can only continue along the course of the river, trusting that one day the fissures and the wounds to our pride, our livelihood, and our loved ones will heal.

As long as there is water in the river, it will move toward the Greater Water.

The river always wins. It is relentless.

The weather is relentless, coming at us every day. Every single day. People used to talk about the weather because it mattered, because their crops and their livelihood depended on it, and so did their survival, economic and otherwise.

They lived with hope and defiance, certain that the rain would come. Someday.

9

The Rains

It does not rain when the dry, broken land is ready. It rains when the rain is ready.

Only when enough drops have gathered can water fall from the sky.

Be ready. Put out rain barrels. Have the seed stored away, the tractor repaired and ready.

The water returns. The rains are coming.

Can we absorb the rain? Are we ready to replenish and move on, or has drought so hardened us that we can no longer feel joy when the grass greens up and the flowers bloom once more? We have to prepare ourselves to move downriver again, to join with the other drops and continue. To soften ourselves to let the water soak in.

It is our nature to be resilient. After the horrors of World War II, the vines and the jungles of the South Sea islands took back the land, overwhelmed the abandoned aircraft and pushed through the concrete landing strips. The machines of war gave way to the lush resilience of nature.

The rains will come again, and the drought ends when *green* becomes a verb.

The land greens up. Progress is not constant, but it is as persistent as native grass in an ancient seedbed, waiting for its chance.

At some point, water falls from the sky. Renewal comes when and where it will. Want it and be ready.

You have to love the rain the way the grass loves

it, the way a dry creek bed loves it. We have to prepare ourselves, soften ourselves, so the returning goodness can soak in, be absorbed, and not run off.

Our culture has become a hardpan, hard-baked place, in desperate need of rain, a slow soul-soaking of human kindness.

And when that water does come down from the sky, it runs toward the sea. The river always, eventually, runs toward it, never away. So, too, does human progress, moving always toward the Greater Water.

The drops have purpose, each one. Be ready for your purpose, prepared to move to the sea.

Flowers are going to bloom again. Hope and defiance put deep roots into the droughty ground looking for moisture, trying to stay alive, to hold on and hang in, and their reward was life itself. They did not perish in the drought.

In 1968, on April 4th and June 6th, respectively, Martin Luther King, Jr., and Robert Kennedy died at the hands of assassins, each from gunshot wounds. Leaders lay dead, leaders of moving waters. A drought descended upon movements of liberation and dignity, but the river continued to seek the sea.

In New York City, on June 28, 1969, a group of gay citizens of the United States of America pushed back against oppression, and the Stonewall uprising signaled that rain had fallen once more on the human spirit. A movement sprang up and with it a harvest, the gay rights movement. Soon came the surging power of the women's movement, and the Chicano rights movement jumped up, roiling and rolling and carving its path. And the ecology movement, later known as the environmental movement, bubbled up from the pages of Rachel Carson's classic 1964 book, *Silent Spring*. The rains had returned, restoring streams and tributaries; drops, more than one, more than a few, gathered and flowed again, enough to wear away the rock, to slough it away and carry it to the sea.

The symbiosis between the sky and the river had been restored, and the hammered, hardened land, growing softer by the hour, sang in joy, the fish spawning and jumping, the cattle and horses raising their voices in harmony, the sound of the earth breathing steady beneath it all.

Such is the goodness of water falling from the sky.

Did we learn anything from the drought, from thirst and scarcity? Did we absorb the dryness? Did it get into and under our skin? Did lessons come with it? We think most often of absorbing moisture, but dryness can get into our souls, and a bitter, mean smallness as well.

We have to prepare ourselves to soften ourselves. We have turned away from the simple gift of being decent people, knowing that it rains on the just and the unjust, yet standing by and watching as it rains wealth on a few today while others parch in drought.

Put out the rain barrels. Harvest the water. There will be enough for all, enough as well for the irrigation ditches and the reservoirs to hold water again, for the river to run.

It will come gradually and then all at once, running always toward and never away from the sea, knowing that there is a Greater Water, that there is some reason.

Reason and the heart, for both are needed. The heart, the spirit, to know the way, and reason, the mind, to find it, to find our way past prejudice and hatred and the dismissive disrespect of refusing to listen.

Prejudice, arrogance, and hatred are like a log-jam that keeps the water from itself, that keeps the river from gaining strength and depth and power. Renewal comes in volumes of water, the rate of flow no longer a trickle, and its ability once again to wear away the rock, to transform and carry it along.

The rain is steady now, a soaking rain, bringing the river and us forward as the water moves clear in its purpose, its drops surging, rushing over all in its path.

It is not our responsibility to create or provide a path, for it will find its own way. Our task is to not impede or pollute it, to allow it to flow clean, to sparkle in the sunlight and cast moonlight back into the night, for when the rains return and the river rushes again, it must rush on now in its own time, its own rhythms, a jazz drummer driving the band, keeping the notes and melody moving through every improvisation all the way through to the last note.

It must flow, for its time is coming.

The water is moving no matter what. It will carry with it wafers of rock, tree limbs, pollutants, good topsoil, plastic bottles, oxygen, fishing line, tiny organisms, and the stories and memories of all who have lived along its banks.

It offers itself just as it has since its headwaters, but you have to choose the river, want the full, diverse life it provides. You can choose to be a dried up, wizened, hardened shell of a person, a bitter cynic convinced that the dawn brings heartbreak and disappointment each day.

You see them. People so parched and cracked open, the fissures in their hearts all the way through to their souls, that if it were to rain on them, it would all run off. Their capacity to absorb would be gone, much less the opportunity to become verdant and bring forth blossoms and renewed life once more.

In Mumbai, India, there is a famous hotel, the Taj. Many years ago, during the monsoon season, there was a report of water streaming down a hallway. The manager sent plumbers and engineers to investigate, but they found no leaks, no ruptured pipes. Rather they found the stream coming from beneath the door of one room. When they entered, they found a man and a broken window. He was from the desert, and he had never seen it rain before, so he took a chair and smashed out the window so that he could know what rain feels like. He stood there, soaked and joyous, knowing and smelling and seeing water fall from the sky. He had waited a lifetime.

10

When Time Calls Your Name

Time and water are the same, for each is made of itself. Each is unique to itself but in need of the other, for time is of water and water is of time.

Seconds are drops.

Minutes, streams.

Hours are tributaries.

Days and weeks and months roll into rivers of time into the Greater Water.

The floods and the droughts have come and gone. There is only now to move forward.

In 1968 the Chambers Brothers sang and

hammered out on a relentless cowbell, "Time Has Come Today." It was an anthem, a declaration, and they were right. It comes every day.

When time calls your name, listen. Answer. Pay attention.

Time has not changed. Our perceptions of time have changed because of technology, but no matter how much you rush forward, the location of the ocean doesn't change. You still have to get there. The shoreline doesn't come toward you. It stays where it is. You have to go to it. You have to get there. No shortcuts. No cutting in line. No free passes. It takes time to wear away the rock. It takes time for drought to scavenge the land. It takes time for the slow rains to heal the earth, to soak deep into the ground to repair the fissures.

It takes time to change hearts. Laws can change in the space of a legislative session, but not so with hearts. There is rule change, and then there is heart change.

After working together to create rule change, if you do no more than learn to respect each other's humanity, that much alone is heart change.

Time is necessary in all this change. There is an old saying: Time is of the essence. That is incorrect. Time is the essence. It is the essence of all things, for all things take place in the sweeping rhythm of seconds.

When the accumulation of seconds has come and gone, and the necessary space has been traversed, the water will reach the mouth of the river, the staging point, where it goes to mix and blend and become enriched.

The space is defined not by the banks of the river but by the watershed and the sky and the distances the clouds travel and the elevations from which the raindrops fall.

Time matters because of what the water had to do along the way, its purpose, its job — ecosystems, drinking water, environmental flows, barge traffic, fishing, food, recreation, contemplation.

There is no substitute for it, no rushing the time it takes for the conjoined drops to carve their own path, and to re-carve, to continually wear away the rock.

You do not suddenly arrive at the sea. The coast waits. It does not rush forward, arms outstretched, happy to see you. You have to bend and flex and work your way past every sandbar and fallen tree, every snag, through every channel. Looking down on a river from an airplane, you see its bendy and twisty path.

Because the river is a living, breathing, dynamic being, time becomes even more important because time is the same as the water. Time does not run straight. If it did, there would be no "déjà vu," no memories, no futures imagined, no dreams. That is its magic, its illusory hold on us. Time does not march on, it moves on and not always smoothly. Our lives double back on themselves, and we see both our past and our future while standing in the middle of the bend in the river.

In fact, the water and time together require a final step: the estuary.

Time is a living creature that winds itself upon itself, enfolding us in its snags and our mistakes, situations we have found ourselves in before. It is a topic of broad and eternal interest:

> Bide your time.
> Take your time.
> Make time.
> Find time.
> Time after time.
> Time's a wastin'.
> A limited-time offer.
> No time like the present.

The takes on time are as widespread as the uses of water.

It serves a purpose just as the movement of water does. Nourishes us, provides a marker, provides the time-space to operate in, as relentless as the river. Not a gentle stream, nothing rolls forward so much as time and the river, rolling together to a final step, one neither can take without the other. The estuary.

Water and time together require it, for without the estuary there is no Greater Water, neither its beginning nor its continuing.

11

The Estuary

Let it cook.

This, the estuary, where fresh water and salt water meet, this is where life began. Science tells us that here, in these tide pools, life began in a blending of cosmic proportions. This is where it mixed and got good, thick and close, the unfamiliar now familiar, murky and slow, varied and diverse. The estuary does not let the water rush forward. It lets it cook, like a fine gumbo.

The best gumbo comes from a good roux, the stock or sauce of the dish. It comes not from a recipe but from experience. Get the roux right, add the ingredients, and then do one thing— let it cook.

Don't fuss over it. Turn down the burner and get out of the way. From the confluence, the coming together, the bubbling and the swirling, comes the richness, the goodness, the flavor, a new form of something greater than the sum of all its parts. Let it cook.

This is where it all comes together, a place where all things, all life forms, are possible and unexpected. It comes from the simmering and the melding as old drops, come now so far, soak up new possibilities in an unfamiliar place in order to prepare for the shock of the salt and the waves and the endless currents.

In this long process of trusting and evolving, all things, all life forms, are possible. After all, the fresh water is about to meet its saline cousin and ride on unceasing waves, provide life for the whole planet and a home for creatures it has not yet imagined.

Thick and close and unfamiliar, murky and

slow, varied and diverse, the estuary does not let the water rush on. It makes it slow down. Makes it richer.

No recipe, no list of ingredients in a primordial cookbook dictates nor even suggests this process but rather a long, bubbling, bathing, moving, intermingling, squishing, and settling of all that has been borne to the mouth of the river by each drop, every drop, carried down from the headwaters to this final step before entering the Greater Water.

It is not exact, it is not industrial, nor formulaic. Yet it is science, for it is discovery and a trusting observance of a method, an experiment, a hopeful process, and a blessed accident.

The good stuff—tacos and bicycles and baseball and Aretha, and whatever else invents itself in the blessed muck of this cosmic happening—can be understood only in part by science. The good stuff jumped up and took hold of its chance at life because an eclectic mix of ingredients happened to be present and equally as well because there was no time limit. Without time, the estuary cannot cook, cannot blend and become what it is. Each batch has the chance to turn out however it will, for the ingredients are never quite the same, except for two—the fresh and the salt.

In this place, this leg of the journey, the fresh water finds the salt water, and together they create new forms.

And what comes of that? Life. Life comes from that.

Let it cook.

This is the last stop before the Greater Water. Give up limits and boundaries and old notions and crumbling structures in order to move into the currents and the depths, the swells and the tides.

Just as the river needed each drop in order to come into being, to thrive, so too does the Greater Water need each drop to become enriched, rested, and ready for all that is to come. Reflect now on all that has been experienced and endured, from which much can be offered to the Greater Water. This is where the vitality of new life comes from, from the slow simmer and the mingling of flavors, the spices and smells of infusions of low heat and a cook with a light touch, whether the old forms and beings like it or not.

The estuary becomes a delta, spreading itself, spilling itself into a broad, shallow fan, disgorging itself of all the rock and dirt and soil and detritus before it moves on. It will lay those burdens down before it takes on the salt, transforming and stepping away from its carved and chiseled bed into the deeper troughs, canyons, and trenches of the ocean floor.

That drop carried its load. Done with that, did

that, wore away the rock and carried its particles all the way downriver. Watered the livestock, nurtured the crops, carried the freight, offered drinking water, gave a place to paddle a canoe, spun the turbines of hydroelectric power, provided a place for a bear to catch a salmon and a grandfather to teach a grandchild to fish.

Give that up. Be done. Leave it behind. You did that, you carried your load, you wore away the rock and carried its particles with you all the way downriver. Become, now. Room to roam now, depths to explore, currents to cruise in a place vast and yet constantly renewed by the presence of each and every new drop.

Become water once more, leaving behind the sloughed, flaked rock to become water once again, to become part of the Greater Water. Become, now.

12

The Greater Water

Actually, the destination does matter.

Yes, the journey matters, but so does the destination. If you keep going toward the Greater Water, you will eventually reach a place that joins you with other drops that have come from all the headwaters.

All those drops, each with its own journey, its own narrative, churn and splash together, pulled by forces larger than the sum of all the drops. Powerful currents, bigger and faster than any river on land, circle the globe, work in harmony with the moon to swing tides that influence the weather, shipping, commerce, geopolitics, and every life on the planet.

And what do the drops learn from this? They learn to move with purpose toward goodness and that the journey has been worth it, even the floods and the rapids and the drought. They learn that there is progress and hope in all things human and that time is not an ultimate measure. The drops learn that the culmination of this long, arduous way is the knowledge that they are just getting started, and that we guide ourselves with both the newest technology, so that we can adjust our course, and as well with our eye on the North Star, under whose guidance the ancients traveled.

The drops learn as well the simple truth that without the ocean, without such a place to balance and maintain life systems, humanity would perish.

If the ocean dies, we die. Our journey ends.

For now, we continue. Undertows and rip-tides and jet streams move drops in ways never imagined while in the river. Peaceful? Restful?

No. The Greater Water is dynamic and powerful, and it moves. And what do the drops learn from this ride on the tide? That the destination is not what they expected, and the journey gets even better.

The drops, free now, have moved on to a place unique to itself but part of something greater than itself.

And yet, as vast as the ocean is, it is in truth a big thing on a small, vain planet.

The Greater Water has taken the beating of degradation, of oil spills and the depletion of fishing stocks, the blood and sunken dead of wars, the scars of enslavement and human trafficking, the pollution of discharged bilges and sewage, miles of trash and plastic, and has endured the ultimate arrogance of being taken for granted.

Yet it persists, knowing that it is depleted and polluted and yet providing life and sustenance, for it lives on many levels, knows it has been compromised but never misses a tide, never denies a wave the right to break on the shore, more necessary than ever before, needed to feed the world and to provide us with the reassurance of the tides and waves, which keep coming, keep coming, the chorus of an eternal song of life together.

Our ancestors turned to the sea for food and trade, for dreams of faraway places.

Immigrants crossed the waters to reach new lands, to catch sight of the Statue of Liberty.

Now we look to the sea for the possibility of desalinated water, electrical power from offshore turbines, and, if we are smart about it, an ongoing supply of sustenance.

Even more, the Greater Water provides a place for our longings, the universal desire for a place better than this present world we have created.

Each evening people gather on beaches around the world, not only for the beauty of the sunset but because the sun over the water is so far beyond our selves that a person can imagine that there is room between here and there for our souls, for hope between the sunset and the sunrise in the east twelve hours later.

This collection of drops stretching to the horizon, the coalescing of the drops from all the rivers, is not a placid rest but an adventure and an invitation.

Come on! Let's go!

We're free now! Come on!

We're part of the Greater Water and on the way to it at the same time.

Eternal rest is to be found in moving on, in constant motion—surfers on a long slow curl into the ether.

The sun is always shining on the ocean some-where. Drops, timeless and salty, infused from the estuary, cruise on the currents, free to be borne through and across a liquid world rich in a promise of future places never expected nor even imagined.

There is no future without the ocean, without water, without the Greater Water that exists at once on infinite levels, sustaining our bodies and our spirits. The Greater Water is the cul-mination, the desire sought and expressed, the sirens' song without the shipwreck.

Hope and progress now must enlist the drops of the world to sustain life itself. Our culture has taught us that there is nothing greater than our own selves. It is a lesson in smallness. Life is long, and large.

The present and the future are one and the same, and the past is as varied as life under the sea. The drops have come down from the headwaters through a chiseled course to the Greater Water, which is reward but also preparation, for nothing yet is done.

A drop and more drops fly through the water to new places, to cycles of continuation, as circular as the globe and the currents that traverse it. Moving on with constant purpose, eternal in their movement, they surge out to sea.

A storm gathers on the far horizon.

The River Always Wins

Eight hundred miles off the coast of Africa, currents churn the surface of the Atlantic. The water chops and collides and dances as it has since forever.

A storm gathers above. High pressures and low pressures bang off one another, and the sky twists itself into iron fists of green vapor.

Lightning breaks as caps of gray-white foam jet up from the roiling sea.

The waves jump, the wind shrieks, and the storm grows until chutes of water leap off the crests as though aspiring to join the heavens.

And some do. Some of the drops leaping highest

fly up into the storm as it gathers water and power and begins to churn and spin and rotate, its path now set on whatever happens to be in its way.

It heads for land because the land is in its path and without ego or will or forethought it simply moves toward the American lands, lashing and pummeling everything that happens to exist along its path.

At last, far inland, the storm begins to play out.

A drop of rain that danced up from the crest of a wave and found itself lifted into the storm now rises 40,000 feet into the air. Along the way it sheds its earthly salt as its pure liquid essence hurtles upward, and then, at a point determined by wind and altitude and the terrain below, begins to fall. It freezes and thaws three times on the way down before it lands without ceremony upon the earth.

It rolls into a slim crevice where stone and tree

root hang tight together on a hillside, and it begins its way down. It travels alone. Through rock and dirt and roots it falls as gravity pulls it like a man sliding down a steep incline unsure of how he will stop.

At last it comes to a ledge and rolls onto its lip and elongates as it dangles in a last moment of solitude.

Below are other drops, many of them, an underground stream that rolls, clear and cold, onward and down.

The drop's own weight eases it down into the current of the subterranean flow, which accepts it and welcomes it, and together the stream continues the long journey of filtration and purification as the drops move together toward their destination — the headwaters.

And so the river lives. It begins again with just one drop. More drops fall, joining together until enough have gathered to rise up from their caverns and rock hollows and aquifers, each drop still its own, individual, but together finding their way to daylight yet again.

In so doing, in place and means and time, the river begins again. And in so doing, in beginning again, the river wins. It always does.

La Reunion Publishing is an imprint of Deep Vellum established in 2019 to share the stories of the people and places of Texas. La Reunion is named after the utopian socialist colony founded by Frenchman Victor Considerant on the west bank of the Trinity River across from the then-fledgling town of Dallas in 1855. Considerant considered Texas as the promised land: a land of unbridled and unparalleled opportunity, with its story yet to be written, and the La Reunion settlers added an international mindset and pioneering spirit that is still reflected in Dallas, and across Texas, today. La Reunion publishes books that explore the story of Texas from all sides, critically engaging with the myths, histories, and the untold stories that make Texas the land of literature come to life.